Learn about Reindeer

Katie Peters

GRL Consultant Diane Craig,
Certified Literacy Specialist

Lerner Publications ◆ Minneapolis

Note from a GRL Consultant
This Pull Ahead leveled book has been carefully designed for beginning readers. A team of guided reading literacy experts has reviewed and leveled the book to ensure readers pull ahead and experience success.

Lerner Publications
An imprint of Lerner Publishing Group, Inc.
241 First Avenue North
Minneapolis, MN 55401 USA

For reading levels and more information, look up this title at www.lernerbooks.com.

Main body text set in Memphis Pro 24/39
Typeface provided by Linotype.

Photo Acknowledgments
The images in this book are used with the permission of: © eyeCatchLight Photography/Shutterstock Images, p. 3; © Menno Schaefer/Shutterstock Images, pp. 4–5; © Agnieszka Bacal/Shutterstock Images, pp. 6–7; © Jeff McGraw/Shutterstock Images, pp. 8–9, 16 (left); © Andre Coetzer/Shutterstock Images, pp. 10–11; © Kjoland/iStockphoto, pp. 12–13, 16 (right); © Charlton Buttigieg/iStockphoto, pp. 14–15, 16 (center).

Front cover: © Ghost Bear/Shutterstock Images

Library of Congress Cataloging-in-Publication Data

Names: Peters, Katie, author.
Title: Learn about reindeer / Katie Peters.
Description: Minneapolis : Lerner Publications, [2025] | Series: Let's look at polar animals (pull ahead readers - nonfiction) | Includes index. | Audience: Ages 4–7 | Audience: Grades K–1 | Summary: "Reindeer are a type of deer, and they are also called caribou. Leveled text and full-color photographs help readers learn more fun facts about these well-known creatures. Pairs with the fiction text, Reindeer Hooves"— Provided by publisher.
Identifiers: LCCN 2023031871 (print) | LCCN 2023031872 (ebook) | ISBN 9798765626320 (library binding) | ISBN 9798765629307 (paperback) | ISBN 9798765634608 (epub)
Subjects: LCSH: Reindeer—Juvenile literature.
Classification: LCC QL737.U55 P465 2025 (print) | LCC QL737.U55 (ebook) | DDC 599.65/8—dc23/eng/20230804

LC record available at https://lccn.loc.gov/2023031871
LC ebook record available at https://lccn.loc.gov/2023031872

Manufactured in the United States of America
1 – CG – 7/15/24

Table of Contents

Learn about Reindeer

Reindeer are a kind of deer.

They are also called caribou.

Reindeer have antlers on their heads.

The antlers fall off each year.
Then new ones grow.

Reindeer live in big groups called herds.

They eat grass and moss.

Did You See It?

antlers

grass

herd

Index